Advent Prayers for Kids

LUISETTE KRAAL

Copyright © 2022
These prayers can be freely copied and shared.
If used for commercial use, please email saved.serve@gmail.com for written permission.
Publisher: Saved to Serve International Ministry
Fishes design: Yayamini

Dedication

This book is dedicated Ashley Jimena Cantu, our newest friend in Iglesia Cristiana La Vid, and all the families from Park Community Church serving God faithfully together.

Merry Christmas.

Feliz Navidad

The Lord is near. Hold fast and pray.

Introduction

Why is a Christmas book decorated with fishes?

The fish (ichthys) historically was a symbol for Christians to meet in a safe place. In the Romans' times, the church was persecuted; that is the word we use to say that the police would take the Christians to prison because it was against the law to pray to Jesus. When Christians wanted to pray in a group, they used this symbol so other Christians would know where to look for other believers and find people to pray with but still be safe.

The word "Ichthys" comes from Greek.

It is an acrostic and can be read as:

> I – Iota (which means Jesus)
> X – Christos (which means Christ)
> N – Theou (which means God)
> Y – Yidos (which means Son)
> Y – Sigma (which means Savior).
> If you put it all together, it means

"Jesus Christ, God's Son, is Savior."

Let's pray.

CONTENTS

Hope..1

Prophet's Candle..3

    1. Christmas Hope 4

    2. Trusting God in Hope..5

    3. Hope for loving others..6

    4. To have hope..7

    5. To Hope Patiently...8

    6. Hopeful Family 9

    7. Hope in God for a Miracle..10

Faith..11

Bethlehem's Candle...13

    8. Faith..14

    9. Faith for Friends...15

    10. Faith to Overcome..16

    11. Faith to Give...17

    12. Faith and not Fear..18

    13. Faith when Afraid...19

    14. Faith for tomorrow..20

Joy..21

Shepherd's Candle...23

    15. Christmas Joy..24

    16. Joy in Caring and Sharing..25

    17. Joyful in Jesus' Love..26

19. Joy with Family Treats...27

20. Joy with Grandparents..28

21. Joy because of Parents...29

15. Joy to Prepare the Home..30

Love/Peace...**31**

Angel's Candle..33

22. Candle in Bethlehem..34

23. To have peace in You...35

24. Angels Candle..36

25. To have love...37

26. Love your Enemies..38

27. Christmas Presents..39

28. Jesus second coming...40

Week 1

Hope

Prophet's Candle

Prophet's Candle

It is Advent. It is time to prepare our hearts for Christmas. We celebrate that Jesus came into the world. This good news was already shared all the way back in the Old Testament when the Prophet Isaiah spoke about Jesus coming into the world. You see, our HOPE is Jesus. During the first week of Advent, we think about hope. If we light a candle, we call this candle HOPE. To hope in God is another way to say we trust in God. We know for sure that when we pray, God hears us and wants to help us. Let's pray every day, one of the Hope-Prayers.

"Christmas Hope"

Dear God,
Thank you for sending our Messiah, Jesus, the only reason,
For this beautiful celebration of the advent season.
We remember, Your child has been born on earth,
Because to You, we have so much worth.
Isaiah announced the Messiah to arrive,
so all the world can have everlasting life.
Because You from heaven has sent Your Son to us,
We wait in hope for our Savior, the Lord Jesus.
Help us to pray for our neighbors and all others,
You are our Father, so we are all sisters and brothers.

In Jesus' name, we pray.

"Trusting God in Hope"

Dear God,
I will trust you with all my heart,
And from you, I will never part.
Mommy and daddy tell me not to worry.
Sometimes I do, but I am sorry.
Jesus, I trust you and will try not to fear,
Because of your grace, you are always so near.
You are my helper and my friend.
I will trust you till the very end.
All-day, my family and I, You protect.
For this, we owe you so much respect.
Every night you put me to rest.

Jesus, you are the best!
Amen!

"Hope for loving others"

Dear God,
Help me to be kind and to always share,
Because that is how we show others we care.
Whether we are tall or small,
You are there to help us all.
You walked so far to help the sick,
And they got better real quick.
I want to be of help to you too,
And grow up to be just like you.
Help me to always be good,
to everyone in my neighborhood.
But even when I am out of place,
Help me to depend on your grace.
I pray for you to help me do better
And receive forgiveness altogether.
You are so good in every way.
Help me to always obey.
God, with all my heart, I love you.
Help me to love others too.
In Jesus' name, I pray.

Amen

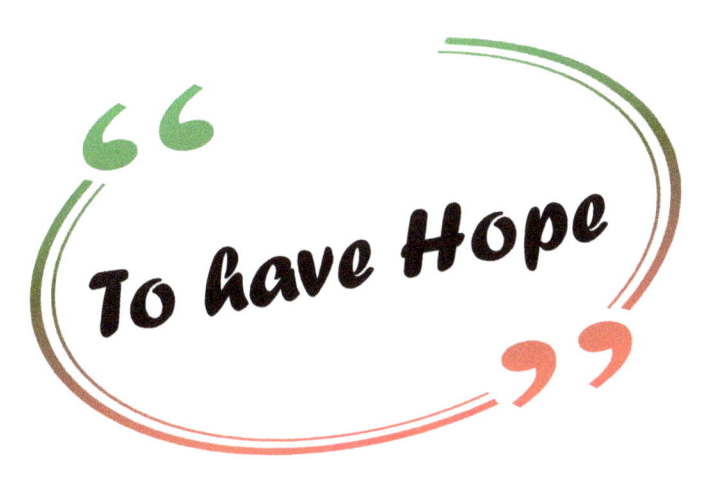

To have Hope

Dear God,
Now and then, I cry at night,
But in the morning, everything is alright.
Even when I find it hard to cope,
You always help me to have hope.
Though sometimes there is a disaster,
You still fill us with joy and laughter.
You said you will come again,
So I know I won't wait in vain.
Jesus, I hope to meet you one day,
And by your side,

I will stay.
Amen

"To Hope Patiently"

Dear God,
You tell me everything will be alright.
Even if at home there is a fuss or a fight.
I know; you are always ready,
and will help keep me steady.
God, I know you are always waiting,
To let me have fun when I'm playing
During recess, when it's swing time,
Let me wait patiently in line.
Help me not to cry myself to sleep,
Just because daddy didn't give me a treat.
Let me hope and trust each day,
In your loving name, I pray.
Amen.

"Hopeful Family"

Dear God,
As a family, we gather to pray,
giving thanks to you every day.
Our prayers you hear,
God, you are always near.
For my family, you protect and provide
May we be always faithful by your side.
Mommy and Daddy tell me you are so caring.
My loving parents are always sharing.
Many people I know live so far,
help them to know how near you are.
I wish I could show them with a big telescope.
In the end, in your heaven, we all have to hope!
Please let my entire family follow your way.
Please, Lord, help them also to always pray.
In Jesus' name, Amen.

"Hope in God for a Miracle"

Dear God,
Miracles God You always do,
You want to do miracles for me too.
Right now, as I lay down sing and praise,
The constellations are still moving in their place.
God makes the fish breathe underwater,
And a mother gives birth to a son or daughter.
Even the flowers have the finest clothes.
Just look at a beautiful blooming red rose.
It is a miracle that You count the hairs on my head.
And that every morning You wake me out of bed.
Today I put my hope in you, Lord,
And my family and I sit in one accord.
And we pray,
In Jesus' name, Amen.

Week 2

Faith
Bethlehem's Candle

Bethlehem's Candle

This week we will pray with faithto the Lord. We call this candle the "Bethlehem's Candle." The prophet Micah foretold that the Messiah would be born in Bethlehem. Jesus was born in the same city as King David.

"Faith"

God, please help me to believe.
You say a mustard seed faith is all I need.
When I pray and believe,
The Bible tells me; I will receive.
I pray today; I will never doubt,
Because you tell me things will work out.
You say, many blessings will follow me,
I believe, even though the future I cannot see.
God, nothing is too hard for You.
I know the great things You can do.
Amen.

"Faith for Friends"

Dear God,
Thank you for sticking close.
This is what I love the most.
You are a friend indeed,
And everything I need.
Help me to be good to my besties,
And also pray for my enemies.
My friends and I are a team.
Let us not choose to be mean.
Thank you for all my friends.
Let our friendship never ends.
I pray we will help each other,
Stick together as a brother.
Jesus, I love you,
And all my friends too.
Amen.

"Faith to Overcome"

Lord teach me not to give in to sin,
I know that is not the way to win.
Even if someone makes me cry,
help me to quickly look up to the sky.
Jesus keep me from all strife,
Thank you for giving me life,
Help me to be peaceful and not wild,
Just because I am your child,
Under your protection, I want to stay
In Jesus name I pray.
Amen.

"Faith to Give"

Dear God,
Help me to give and to share,
That shows others how much I care.
Let me give a hug to friends who are sad,
That will brighten their day and make them glad.
I can also give something I wear,
That does not have a stain or tear.
There is a lot of giving during this season.
You gave us your Son; that is a good reason.
I pray I can have faith in you all the days,
And that I can give with a heart full of praise.
In Jesus' name, Amen.

"Faith and not Fear"

Dear God,
I remember that little David won Goliath with a sling.
That is why, as a family, tonight, we can sing.
I will not be afraid of visible enemies
Or look under the bed for imaginaries.
Giants and monsters, I should not fear,
for You are always near.
Even though size is intimidating,
God, your strength is never failing.
You are so big and wise,
It doesn't matter my size.
Even when I am afraid of a giant
I can trust you because you are brilliant.
Lord, you give me faith to believe,
If I don't, your spirit I will grieve.
In faith, I bow my head to pray,
Trusting you day by day.
In Jesus' name,
Amen

"Faith when Afraid"

Dear God,
In this week we celebrate faith in You,
Trusting you is exactly what I want to do.
Thank you for protecting me.
Full of faith, that is how I want to be.
At nights, when the lights go out,
Help me not to panic and shout.
Anytime I feel sad and scared,
I think of what the cross declared.
On this pillow, my head is laid,
Help me, Lord, not to be afraid.
From now on, this is how I want to pray,
Having a greater faith each day.
In Jesus Name,
Amen.

"Faith for tomorrow"

Dear God,
I always worry about tomorrow,
What if it is a day of sorrow?
Thank you for reminding me to put my hope in you.
To trust and have faith that you will see us through.
Thank you that my future is in your hand,
And my family and I are a part of your plan.
As we serve you day after day,
We want to be faithful and always pray.
In Jesus' name,
Amen

Week 3

Joy

Shepherd's Candle

Shepherd's Candle

This week we celebrate the advent week of Joy. We are joyful because we are preparing to celebrate Jesus' birth. When the angles came from heaven to announce Jesus was born, they went first to the shepherds! That is why we call the candle of the 3rd week the "Shepherd's Candle." Jesus coming was first told to humble, simple people. Because that is how God wanted us to know that although Jesus was a King, he came to earth first for humble people who put their trust in Jesus.

Christmas Joy

At Christmas we celebrate,
Jesus, who was born for our sake.
He brings so much joy,
To every girl and boy.
For everyone Jesus came,
Even the sick and the lame.
What great joy the Savior brings,
To his children, he takes good things.
The joy of Jesus' birth has come.
You promised it for all, not just some.
Jesus is here for me and you,
And people who are unkind too.
Whether we are rich or poor,
Jesus is knocking on our heart's door.
Amen

Joy in Caring and Sharing

Thank you, Lord, for being so kind.
You always have me on your mind.
Let me to be kind and share my toys,
With my siblings or other girls and boys.
Help me not to be mean,
Make my heart good and clean.
You love people who even do bad.
When I love them, it makes you glad.
Please help me to deeply care,
For my family, my church, and people everywhere.
Amen.

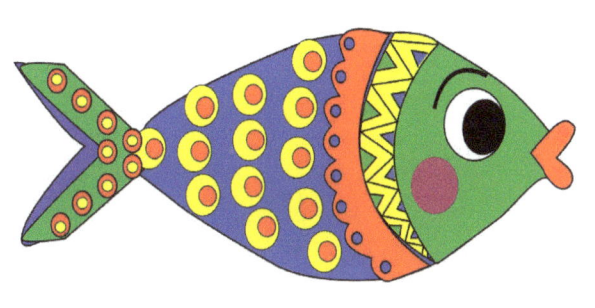

Joyful in Jesus' Love

Jesus loves me and you.
He loves the whole world too.
He gave me loving family members.
To celebrate Christmas full of pleasures.
Praying to Jesus is so cool,
He came to the world to rule.
I am happy to be used as His tool.
Sharing His love is so cool.
Help us to tell everyone how loving you are,
Help us to share it boldly, near, and far.
Remind me what the angels did sing and shout.
So that I will remember what Christmas is about.
In Jesus Name, we pray,
Amen

Joy with Family Treats

Early on the day of Christmas morn,
We celebrate that Jesus was born,
As a family, we pray,
Thanking God for another day.
The story of Bethlehem never gets old,
No matter how many times it has been told.
I help to bake cookies with mommy,
And help to make lasagna with daddy.
Helping to cook is so much fun,
The table is full of the food that is done.
The doorbell gives a welcoming chime,
And my extended family gathers to dine.
We listen to music and eat treats,
And dance to the rhythm of the beats.
Thank you for tasty food and so much more,
Help us Jesus, to be a blessing to the poor.
Thank you, Jesus, for the sweet days.
You love us in so many ways.
Amen

Joy with Grandparents

Thank you, God, for my grandparents.
On Christmas day they give me presents.
Grandpa reads me a story on his rocking chair.
He tells me that for everyone you care.
Grandma tells me to listen to mommy and daddy,
And you will lengthen our lives and make us happy.
Even though they say they are getting old,
Their hugs keep me warm when I am cold.
I want to be with my Gramps forever.
Please help us all to stay together.
God, I ask you to be with them every day.
Thank you, that, to an ageless God, I can pray.
Amen.

Joy because of Parents

Dear God,
Thank you for mommy and daddy.
They love me and make me so very happy.
I pray you continue to help them,
when they face a big or small problem.
The Bible says to follow my parents and obey,
help me to be good to them in every way.
I want to respect my parents and be wise.
For this, you will give a long-life as a prize.
Mommy and daddy give me so much love.
I am thankful you sent them from above.
Please teach me to listen to what they say,
In your holy name, I pray.
Amen.

Joy to Prepare the Home

Get all the beautiful ornaments,
And fill the home with sweet scents.
Put up pretty, ruffled drapes,
And make juicy fruit bowls with grapes.
Turn off the tv-cartoons,
And blow up the balloons.
Arrange the tables and chairs,
For the party downstairs.
When the work is all done,
The fun has just begun!
Then daddy tells us a beautiful story,
of Jesus and His great glory.
Lord, I pray to you with joy in my heart,
As we prepare for this celebration to start.
In Jesus' name,
Amen

Week 4

Love/Peace

Angel's Candle

Angel's Candle

This week we are very close to Christmas already. Our prayers will focus on Peace and Love. Our candle is called the "Angel's Candle." The angels announced that Jesus came to bring peace. He came to bring people close to God and to each other again.

"Candle in Bethlehem"

Everyone began to prepare,
Because baby Jesus was there.
He was born in a city called Bethlehem.
This was first told to three wise men.
They were shepherds who saw angels in the pasture.
A bright star these men went after.
To fulfill God's purpose, Jesus came,
And for all our sins, he took the blame.
That is why today, with our last candle,
We pray because there is nothing our Jesus can't handle.
Amen!

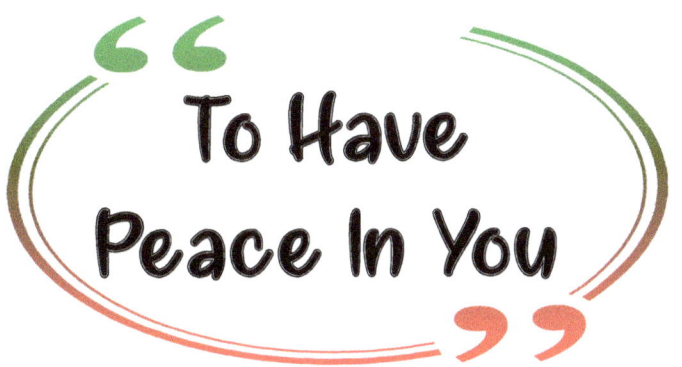
"To Have Peace In You"

Dear God,
Thank you for the peace you give,
Without it, we wouldn't want to live.
In times of sorrow and sadness,
I pray for peace and gladness.
When things make me upset,
Help me not to worry and fret.
Let me have peace,
And let all anger cease.
The peace we receive from your hand,
Is more than we can understand.
Thank you Lord,
Amen.

"ANGELS CANDLE"

Jesus came to bring us close together,
So that we can love one another way better.
Sadly, there may be some fuss and fights,
But with this candle, I remember Christ is the light,
The angels shared Jesus' message of peace,
With grace and love, He puts us at ease
Because of his grace, one day, fighting will cease.
We know that just before Jesus was born,
The night sky lit up like morn.
There the angels started to sing,
Praises to the newborn king.
That is why tonight as I prepare to sleep,
Your peace, please help me to keep.
We thank you that when we celebrate Jesus' birth and life,
We are encouraged to live without anger and strife.
In our hearts, we pray for a new beginning,
As we approach Christmas with thanksgiving.
Amen.

God, you are so loving and kind.
That is why I serve you with all my heart and mind.
Loving others is your golden rule.
You first loved us; you are so cool.
Showing love to others makes me glad,
But if someone is unkind, it makes me sad.
Please help other children to love as you do.
Let me be more like you too.
Jesus, you made the world a better place,
When you died for the whole human race.
Red, yellow, black or white,
All are precious in your sight.
Help me, the good news, always to share,
With friends and families everywhere.
Gifts and Santa should never be higher,
Than the angels message about the Messiah.
Today I pray for the real Christmas to come,
Because we know where the Good News is from.
Amen.

"Love your Enemies"

Dear God,
Please don't let bully's win.
I know what they are doing is a sin.
Jezebel bullied Naboth to get his land.
Her punishment was terrible from your hand.
Help me to always be gentle and loving,
Instead of someone who is pushing and shoving.
If I get bullied at school,
Help me not to break your rule.
I know fighting back is not right.
You are pleased when I am peaceful at night.
Amen.

"Christmas Presents"

Happy times is here again.
The best time of the year my friend.
Dolls and new dresses for the girls,
Because they love to dance and twirl.
Boys receive racing cars and building blocks.
They love to drive and build cool stuff.
Wonderful presents are given to us.
But the best is the gift of baby Jesus.

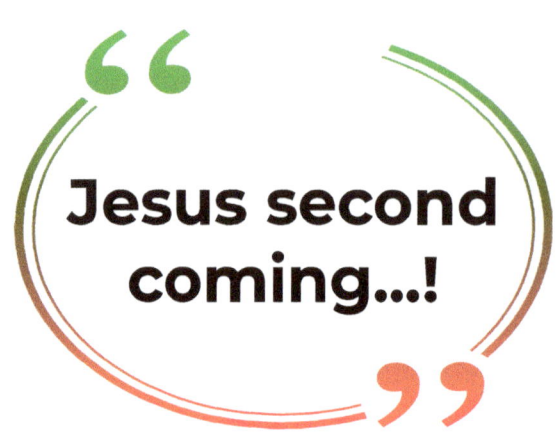

"Jesus second coming...!"

He's coming back soon,
like a bride awaiting her groom.
In hard times, believe and trust,
That one-day, Emmanuel will rescue us.
At first, he came as a baby wrapped in swaddling clothes.
Thirty-three years after, on the third day, He rose.
He will come again not to deal with sin,
But to save those who are waiting for him.

Merry Christmas

THE TALES FROM THE BIBLE
by
LUISETTE KRAAL

The Tale of the
House on the Rock

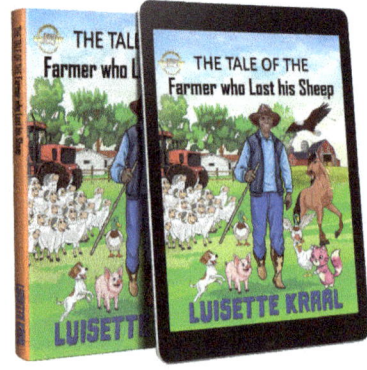

The Tale of the
The Farmer who Lost his Sheep

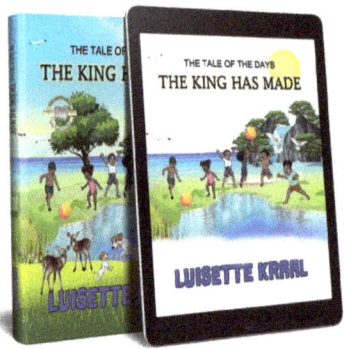

The Tale Of The Days
The King Has Made

The Tale of the
Camel and the Eye of a Needle

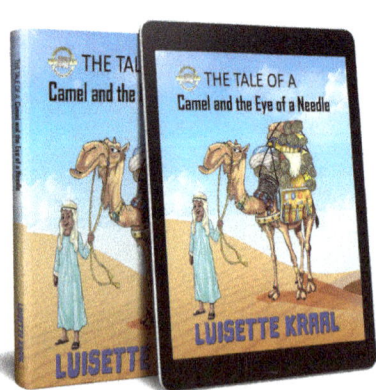

Jonah in the Smelly Belly of the fish

HOPPER
Needs Clean Water

Merry Christmas